THE SALEM WITCH TRIALS

HISTORY 5TH GRADE | Children's History Books

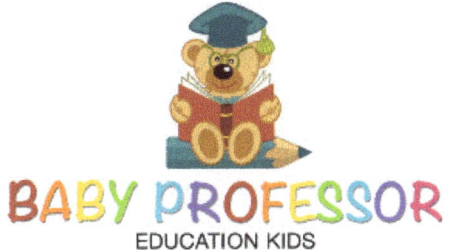

Speedy Publishing LLC

40 E. Main St. #1156

Newark, DE 19711

www.speedypublishing.com

Copyright 2017

All Rights reserved. No part of this book may be reproduced or used in any way or form or by any means whether electronic or mechanical, this means that you cannot record or photocopy any material ideas or tips that are provided in this book

In this book, we're going to talk about the Salem Witch trials. So, let's get right to it!

Centuries ago many people who practiced different forms of Christianity believed that the devil could influence people to behave strangely or commit evil acts. Throughout Europe from the 1300s through the 1600s many thousands of people, mostly women, were accused of practicing witchcraft. If they were found guilty of this devil's magic, they were executed. Eventually, this hysteria over witches stopped in Europe, but then it happened in the British colonies in America.

WHEN DID THE SALEM WITCH TRIALS HAPPEN?

The Salem witch trials happened in the Massachusetts Bay Colony from 1692 to 1693. Over 200 women, men, and children were accused of being witches and 20 were put to death. Later, the colony leaders said that the trials were a tragic error.

DULCIBEL, THE LAST MARCH

They gave money to the families of the accused to compensate them for the grief and agony of losing their loved ones.

E ver since these famous trials the term "witch hunt" is used to describe an event where people are suspicious and accuse others when there's no evidence.

WHAT WAS CAUSING TENSION IN THE MASSACHUSETTS BAY COLONY?

In the year 1689, King William and Queen Mary of England began to fight their enemy France on the lands of the American colonies. This war was called King William's War and it destroyed sections of New York as well as some regions of what is now Canada. Refugees from these areas flooded into Essex County and especially in Salem Village, which was located in the Massachusetts Bay Colony. Today, Salem Village is the city of Danvers.

All these refugees put an enormous strain on the city and its resources. There was already a huge rivalry between families that made their living from the seaport and those who made their living from farming. In addition to the quarreling of these groups, there was another problem.

CITY OF DANVERS

SALEM VILLAGE PARSONAGE FOUNDATION

There was a new ordained minister in the village. His name was Samuel Parris and no one seemed to like him. The citizens who lived in Salem thought he was greedy and very rigid.

They felt that all the distress in the village was the devil's work. It was a tense time and then something happened that made everyone even more scared.

In the first month of 1692, Elizabeth Parris, the minister's daughter as well as his niece Abigail Williams started to have strange "fits" of behavior. They threw things all around, made very strange sounds, and twisted themselves into strange body positions. Elizabeth was 9 years old and Abigail was 11 years old. Ann Putnam, another 11-year-old girl in the village was displaying the bizarre behavior too.

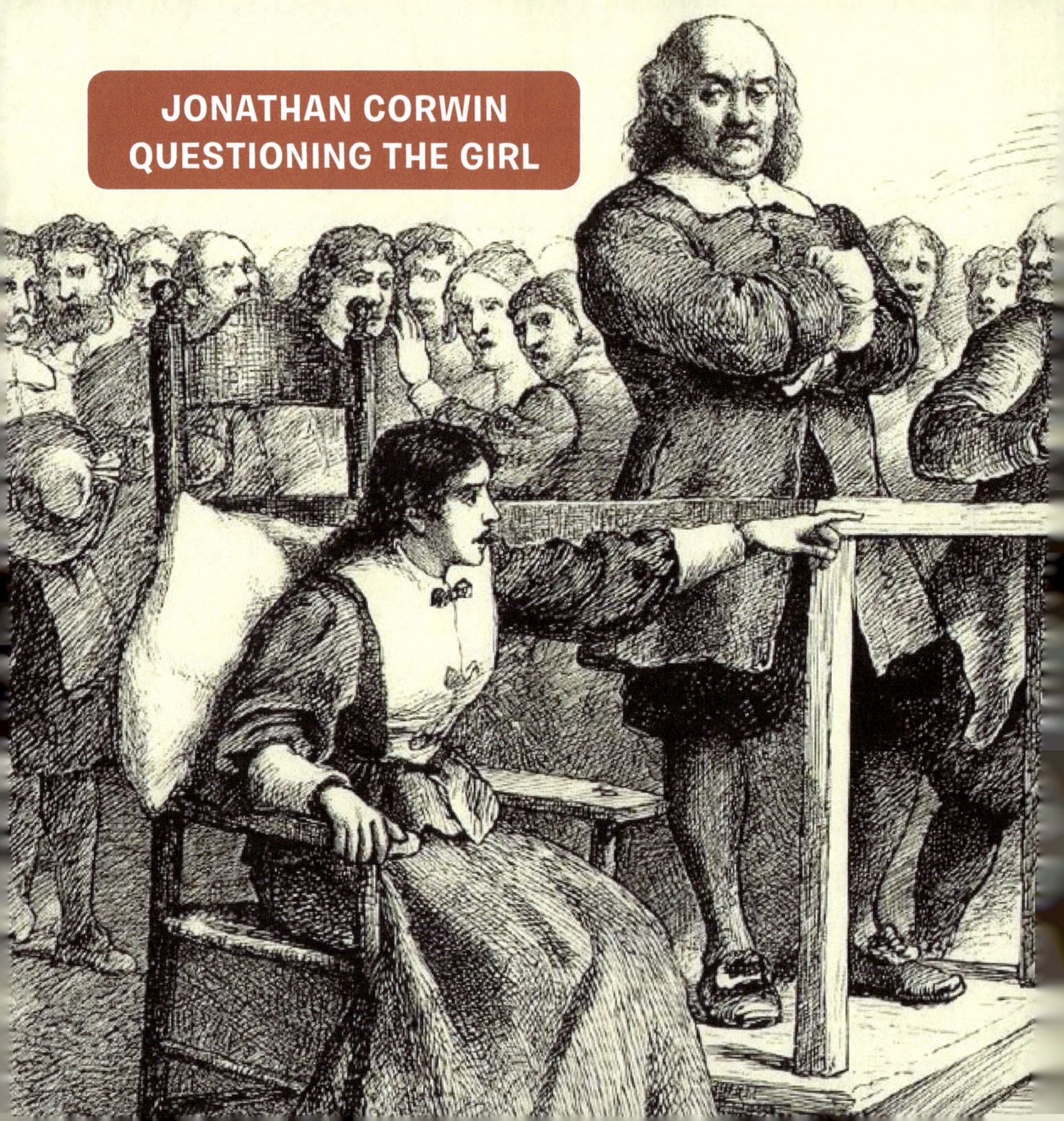

By the end of February, the town's magistrates got involved. The two men, Jonathan Corwin and John Hathorne questioned the girls and the girls gave them three names of women they felt were responsible for their affliction.

They named a Caribbean woman called Tituba, who was working in the Parris home as a slave. They also named Sarah Good who was a beggar wandering the streets and Sarah Osborne, an elderly woman who was poor.

THE WITCH HUNT BEGINS

The women were brought in and questioned over several days beginning on March 1st. Both Sarah Good and Sarah Osborne told the magistrates that they were innocent. However, Tituba said that she had made a deal with the devil. She told an elaborate story of seeing black dogs, cats of red, and yellow birds.

WOMAN JAILED FOR BEING A WITCH

She said that the devil had appeared to her and asked her to sign a book confirming that she would serve him. She told them that she had signed the book willingly and that she was not the only witch who wanted the Puritans destroyed. In her story, she described that she had flown using poles and had baked a "witch's cake." Tituba and the other two women were thrown into jail.

Even though there was no evidence that any of this had happened, Tituba had everyone believing that she was a witch and that anyone, even your next-door neighbor could be a witch.

Over the next months, the accusations flew. Martha Corey who was a devout Church member was accused next.

SALEM WITCH HOUSE

SALEM WITCH TRIAL

The magistrates also questioned Sarah Good's little four-year-old girl, Dorothy. The child was very scared and timid so it looked like she was guilty. By April, news of the trials had spread and Thomas Danforth, the Deputy Governor, and his staff came to the courtroom sessions. Dozens of citizens from Salem as well as from other villages in the surrounding areas were summoned to be interrogated.

SALEM WITCH TRIAL

In May of that same year, William Phipps, the governor of the state created a Special Court of Oyer and Terminer, which essentially meant to hear and decide, the witchcraft cases for three counties. The first case that was brought to trial was Bridget Bishop.

She was a target because she was the town gossip and known for her loose ways. When asked if she was a witch, she said she was an innocent as a child that wasn't

yet born. Despite her protests, she was found guilty and she was executed by hanging on the 10th of June at a place later called Gallows Hill.

COTTON MATHER AND INCREASE MATHER

Five days after Bridget Bishop was hanged, Cotton Mather, who was a minister and highly respected in the community wrote a letter to the court. He requested that testimony regarding dreams and visions not be allowed. In his mind, this type of testimony wasn't evidence. His letter was ignored.

THE ACCUSED WITCHES ARE HANGED TO DEATH

Five people were hanged for witchcraft in July and by the end of September thirteen more people were sentenced and killed. By October 3rd, Cotton's father, Increase Mather, the respected president of Harvard University, pleaded for reason and said that testimony about dreams and visions had no place in a court of law. He stated that it would be better if ten witches were freed than if one person who was innocent was accused and died.

1681
SALEM VILLAGE PARSONAGE

IN 1681 THE SALEM VILLAGE INHABITANTS BUILT A HOME FOR THEIR MINISTER AT THIS SITE. MINISTERS RESIDING HERE WERE: GEORGE BURROUGHS (1681-83), ACCUSED IN 1692 OF BEING A WITCH AND HANGED; DEODAT LAWSON (1684-88), AUTHOR OF THE FIRST VOLUME ABOUT SALEM VILLAGE WITCHCRAFT; SAMUEL PARRIS (1689-96), MINISTER DURING THE WITCHCRAFT HYSTERIA; JOSEPH GREEN (1698-1715), NOTED DIARIST AND AREA PEACEMAKER; PETER CLARK (1717-68), FAMED THEOLOGICAL AUTHOR; AND BENJAMIN WADSWORTH (1772-1826), WHO TORE DOWN THE OLD PARSONAGE IN 1784.

IT WAS IN THIS HOUSE IN 1692 THAT TITUBA, REV. PARRIS' SLAVE, TOLD THE GIRLS OF THE HOUSEHOLD STORIES OF WITCHCRAFT WHICH NURTURED THE VILLAGE WITCHCRAFT HYSTERIA AND RESULTED IN THE DEATHS OF 23 PERSONS. THIS HOUSE WAS THE SCENE OF MANY INCIDENTS DURING THE HYSTERIA, AND IS ONE OF THE MOST IMPORTANT SITES IN COLONIAL AMERICAN HISTORY. ARCHAEOLOGICAL EXCAVATION BEGAN HERE IN 1970.

DANVERS HISTORICAL COMMISSION 1974

GOVERNOR PHIPPS INTERCEDES

The governor responded to Mather's request. The final straw was when the governor's wife was accused and questioned. He stopped the arrests and dissolved the Special Court and replaced it with a Superior Court, which didn't allow evidence from dreams or visions. By May of 1693, the governor released all those who had been accused during the mass hysteria.

However, by then, many lives had been destroyed. Nineteen people had died by hanging on Gallows Hill and an older man had been killed when he was pressed by heavy stones. Several others passed away while they were in prison. Over 200 people had been accused of witchcraft and the "devil's magic" with no evidence that anything had happened at all.

WHAT "TESTS" WERE USED TO DETERMINE IF SOMEONE WAS A WITCH?

If a person was having fits, he or she touched the witch who had supposedly cast the spell. If the person who was bewitched suddenly became calm, it would "prove" that the other person was a witch.

The accusers would dunk an individual in water until the so-called witch confessed to witchcraft. Being underwater like this is torture, so the person might confess just to make it stop.

If the person couldn't say the Lord's Prayer without a mistake, he or she was considered to be a devil follower.

A person could testify that he or she saw the accused person in a dream. In the dream, the accused witch was talking to the devil.

None of these were conclusive evidence and never should have been allowed in a court of law.

WHAT HAPPENED AFTER THE SALEM WITCH TRIALS?

Following the trials, people realized that it had all been a tragic mistake. Many people who had been involved regretted their actions. In 1697, the General Court declared a day of mourning where the citizens of Salem would fast from food and think about the tragedy.

In 1702, the Court stated that the trials hadn't been legal and laws to restore the reputations of the accused and their families were passed.

SALEM TOWNHALL

Money was paid to the heirs of those who had died. However, more than 250 years passed before the state of Massachusetts made a formal apology for the deaths of the "so-called" witches.

In 1976, a psychologist called Linnda Caporael blamed the strange behaviors of the girls on a fungus that is found in rye, wheat, and other cereal grains. She published a paper with her findings.

SUMMARY

It has been over three centuries since the Salem Witch trials happened. To this day, no one is absolutely sure what caused the behavior that was considered witchcraft.

The reason for the "mass hysteria" and the loss of reason that brought about the Salem witch trials is also unknown. The result was the deaths of more than 20 innocent people and suffering to hundreds of others. To this day, when we see an unjust accusation, we call it a "witch hunt."

Now that you know more about the Salem witch trials you may want to find out more about an important journey in the early part of the 17th century in the Baby Professor book Colonial America History for Kids: What Was It Like to Travel in the Mayflower?

Visit

www.BabyProfessorBooks.com

to download Free Baby Professor eBooks and view our catalog of new and exciting Children's Books

Lightning Source UK Ltd.
Milton Keynes UK
UKHW050410051021
391670UK00005B/83

Published by
Speedy Publishing LLC
40 E. Main St., #1156
Newark DE 19711

Cover by 24HR Covers

ISBN 978-1-5419-1228-